The Birthed Wisdom of God

Juliet Onyinyechi

AuthorHouse™
1663 Liberty Drive
Bloomington, IN 47403
www.authorhouse.com
Phone: 833-262-8899

Because of the dynamic nature of the Internet, any web addresses or links contained in this book may have changed since publication and may no longer be valid. The views expressed in this work are solely those of the author and do not necessarily reflect the views of the publisher, and the publisher hereby disclaims any responsibility for them.

Any people depicted in stock imagery provided by Getty Images are models, and such images are being used for illustrative purposes only.
Certain stock imagery © Getty Images.

This book is printed on acid-free paper.

ISBN: 978-1-4520-1432-6 (sc)

Print information available on the last page.

Published by AuthorHouse 03/08/2023

authorHOUSE®

This book is dedicated to the almighty God who alerted me in the spirit to reveal this things.

Preface

Proverb 7:4
Say unto wisdom, Thou art my sister, and all
understanding thy kinswoman.

This Book describes about God's perfect wisdom in
the life we live in this world.

This is an instrument we are not familiar, regarding the things we see, how it is been perceived. The bible said in John 17:16, we are in the world but not of the world. Most of the times, ordinary situations can confuse us in a way we start to look some answers even though we are known to be born-again spirit-filled Christians. Why do we find ourselves in this things? It is because we did not seek God's wisdom regarding those situations. To begin with let me describe the difference between been a born-again Christian and just saying I am a Christian like some of us do. When Jesus met Nicodemus in John 3:5 he said to him unless one is born-again he or she cannot see the kingdom of God. Jesus knows that when one is born of the spirit is different from ordinary Christianity. Because there is a great change in the spirit and life of that person.

But when one is identifying himself or herself as a Christian, you are removing the spiritual part which is what Jesus describes in the bible. The enemy is not only after us physically but spiritually which we all know so when you tell some body that I am a Christian you have practically removed the spiritual part which actually identifies you in the realm of the spirit. So it is very critical, we need to identify our spiritual part most which is the "BORN AGAIN". For example, a person born in the Islamic world claims to be a muslim likewise a hindu person answers Hinduism. When this people receives Christ they become aborn-again of the spirit and water not a religious name like Christian muslim, hindusm. They now belong to Jesus, no longer their religion. That is why the Bible said in the book of prov 1 verse 2 To know wisdom and instruction, To perceive the words of understanding.

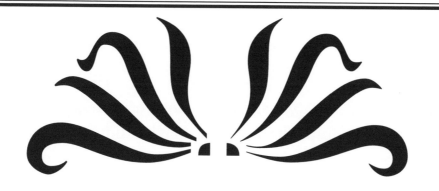

Part I

Wisdom In Childhood

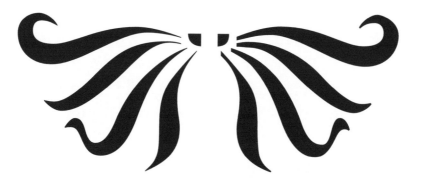

Train up a child the way he should go when he grows up, he will not depart from it.

In the bible king Solomon asked God for an understanding to judge his people. And God gave him that. Remember he did not ask for WISDOM because he was born with wisdom. This means every child or every person is born with wisdom, but not an understanding so it depends which direction you follows in life. There is only one type wisdom and it comes from God himself not from man. Human beings are birthed with wisdom as a child, as they grow, it develops inside of us. The bible says man was made in the image of God, Everyone has a wisdom in them when they were born on the earth. But there was no understanding of the wisdom. The choice of understanding of wisdom comes from God himself if you seek him early. Examples king David through the understanding of the wisdom given to him by God he was able to defeat the king Saul. The bible says he was a man after God's heart. May every problem in your life be defeated by the understanding of the wisdom of God in Jesus name.

The bible says to train a child according to the way they should go when they grow up they will not depart from it. In this situation, God has given us an understanding how to handle our children with the wisdom inside us so that when they grew up, they become someone respectful and useful in the society. It is very good to start early to teach a child the things of God example the word of God, going to services, praying with them at home and let them join congregational choirs. As this individual grows, the knowledge of God will fill them and he will began to long for more, this is when God's understanding will beginging to activate his wisdom. Then they began to make good choices because of the wisdom of God inside them. If a parent or grandparent live by the standard of God's word in their homes, there is always a genuine different in every child raised around that home positively. Most of the time, we parents, grandparents, sisters, uncles, aunt may never know what it means to help a child to developing understanding in order to activate the wisdom inside them. The only way this can be accomplished is if we utilized or live by the standard of the word of God. But if we ignore the things of God, that child began to develop the understanding of satanic wisdom which directs him or her to do the bad stuff. This is very critical, we don't want our children to go to that area. Remember it is only supposed to be one wisdom but in this case this person is controlled by the devil therefore he may not have the chance to use the good wisdom placed inside of him by God. Always pray for your children because they are the generations that make up the world.

Look, if we born-again Christians want our children or grandchildren to walk in the ways pleasing to us, First they need to understand the wisdom of God by obeying the word of God. Example the bible says, Honour they father and they mother so that your days may be long. God knows if we can activate the already wisdom he has put inside every child. They will understand that this is a must in their lives. We spirit filled people need to know how important it is to use the wisdom have in our children or other things but how do we do that in our children- praying over them, reading the scriptures with our kids. Blessing them all the time. You know the Devil does not like this because it keeps him away from our children, from harming them or using them. As a child grows he or she began to embrace the right wisdom.

Part II

God's wisdom in Education

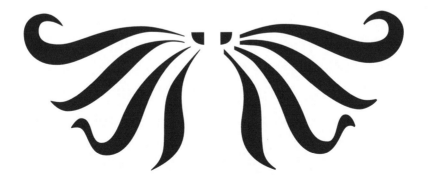

John 7:38:
He that believeth in me shall out of his belly flows
rivers of living water.

Education is one of the key product in our living. What is the bible telling us in this verse? When we agree in the things of God and his son we began to flow spiritually and progress physically. As most of us long to be in different fields – we forget that we need education to be where we want to be. Some of us long to be a lawyer, doctor, nurse, preacher and so forth. It is good but we need the wisdom of God to help us accomplish these in our lives. When we ask God to help us fulfill this purpose, the living water of Jesus flowing inside us make us to have the thirst to fulfill it in our different lives. You see as a born-again not only spiritual thirst for this living water but we also want this living water to bring forth gifts. As we grow in maturity in God, things began to change in the way we perceive or thirst for the things of this world. Education is perfect in our lives and children's lives if it is done in the direction of the Hoy spirit of God. Everything that is perfect comes from God, it does not matter how it does look like but God specializes to make it well. One could flow in rivers of living water out of our belly in those areas we are thirsting for, once we believe in him that gives the living water. Once it starts to flow, it never stops again because it is inside us. As One grows it springs forth and bring about different things or gifts in life. When education is started in the right direction things changes in the home, atmosphere, where we situate ourselves.

The bible says he is like a tree planted in the river side which never withers or dies. As you attend all levels of education in life through the wisdom of God, one definitely have an understanding of what to do with the skills or specialties received. As you believe in Christ Jesus making him the bases of your living, you can accomplish anything you want in this life. We followers of Christ could try to gain enough education in the society, it does not matter what field you are into, it is all education, the world would not look at us as Ignoring school while we follow Jesus. Sometimes we need our children to specialize in a different field for example if you are a preacher, it is God's will to let your youngones to be established in a different area. At the same time allowing the spreading of the gospel through that individual. We cannot never be stuck on one field. What do I mean? Wherever place we find ourselves in education, as far as we are Born-agains we should use it to bring glory to God and as spread the work of Jesus.

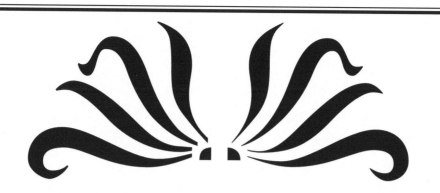

PART III

God's Wisdom In The Church

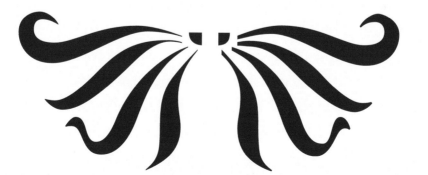

Luke 4:18

The spirit of the lord is upon me because he hath
anointed me to preach the gospel to the poor, he
hath sent me to heal the broken hearted to preach
deliverance to the captives and recovering sight to the
blind, to set at liberty them that are Bruised.

Jesus himself has already shown us the way as preachers, pastors and Bishops. But how can we know how to perform these kind duties in the church if one lacks the understanding of the wisdom in the field. And secondly one needs the anointing of God himself to perform those things. Most churches today are in need of wisdom of God to do the things needed to be accomplish so that the Devil will not have them under attack. In the ministry, there should be the flow of different areas of gifts, with these the pastors will able to function in the ministry. A spirit-filled ministry has already been given the anointing and wisdom to flow in the spirit if they have the understanding of this wisdom inside them. This is where the congregation is needed to pray for these gifts to manifest, the wisdom of Christ is simple. It does not matter how many people are in the ministry or how many services that usually took place, if that wisdom is found there, Everything will begin to transform the church, more work will be completed in a rightful way and organization will be seen among the congregations. Most of all, the sermons will be preached in an organized way under the spirit of God. More souls will come to Christ easily. We really need

God to fill us with understanding of his wisdom instilled in us. You know the enemy does not want the pastors or men of God to use the wisdom of God put inside them to operate in their ministry both physically and spiritually. When this is done, more people come to Christ and more things is accomplished in the kingdom of Christ. So congregation always pray for this gifts for the runners of the ministry.

PART IV

God's Wisdom In Marriage

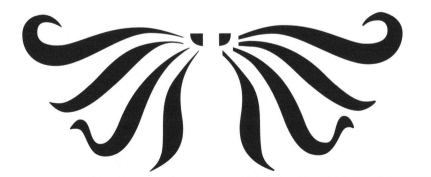

Likewise, ye wives be in subjection to your husbands,
that if any obey not the word, they also may without
the word, they may without one be worn by the
conversation of the wives.

Marriage is a perfect thing if it is done in the wisdom of God.
Sometimes we may not understand the person we are married with, who live
with us, it may be a husband or wife but still we don't understand each other
very well. This is where we need the understanding of wisdom from God that
if it is a man – he was made in the likeness of God as the bible said in genesis.
So a woman should be like Eve – being under a man and embracing him as a
champion or role model in the home. A man being the way he was conformed
need also the wisdom to participate in his role in a household, place of work
especially towards his wife. Most of the time, it is tough to pick out the right
man or woman as a partner in life but if you are a spirit-filled born-again and
ask for the wisdom of God, you will fall in the right direction in making a
good decision. When these happens, the tendency to succeed in marriage and
having a perfect home is very solid. Applying the wisdom of God in marriage
brings out God's plan for married people. In the book of Genesis, the bible
says God created Adam first and seeing he doesn't have a partner, made Eve
from Adam's ribs. Also Jesus said in the new testament that A man will leave
his father and mother and unite with his wife, they no longer shall be two but

one. Therefore what God has joined together no man should put asunder. If we have God's wisdom in our marriages, the chances of divorce will be low. The bible says in proverbs 2-2 So that thou incline thine ear unto wisdom and apply thine heart to understanding. My prayer is that we women will be like what the bible describes as the virtuous woman who does things in the wisdom of God to her husband.

PART V

God's Wisdom In Old Age.

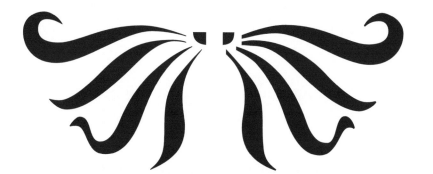

Titus 2:2-3

The bible identifies the work of old men and old women in the ministry, at home as being uniquely different.

As we become older and waxed less strong we definitely need the wisdom of God to strengthen us and to pursue the things of that stage of life. Some times as we get to that point we begin to slow down in certain things as concerning God or mankind. If we have the wisdom in us, this stage is the stage we become more accomplishing in our life. For example walking closer to God and his ministry if one is a pastor or preacher, Holding more crusades if we are privileged to do so in the society. If a preacher continued to preach the gospel at this stage you will begin to experience God's strength in your well being and one will become full of health. For God strengthens his people all the time even in the midst of old age. When old age comes, things changes, at this time one needs to look into certain matters correctly with God's wisdom. It is at this stage that one is expected to leave a good legacy at home, ministry and wherever you find yourself. Including among your peers, in the ministry, children, grandchildren.

Maybe you were a young preacher and during old age then you decide to slow your movement, why slowing down remember this is a walk with the lord to the end. This is when you really need the wisdom to continue your walk with him. Because all those years, you have been preaching, the Devil identifies you in the spirit as one who never tires in his work so during old age he awaits then to see if you will slow down and allow him to ignorantly to take away the strength of God in you. It is better to continue to preach to the end so that he will never have one accountable for anything like laziness. In the book of genesis, the bible says Abraham was the man of faith which was accounted to him as righteousness. This faith man continue to walk with God even during old age. Until he transferred to his children and grandchildren. If we leave a good legacy among our children and grandchildren like Abraham did. He will bless us. As we honour God's words and revelations may we be blessed in our lives in Jesus name Amen.

Printed in the United States
by Baker & Taylor Publisher Services